THE ACCIDENT:
July 21, 1960

by Bob Grudle

RoseDog Books
PITTSBURGH, PENNSYLVANIA 15238

RoseDog Books
585 Alpha Drive, Suite 103
Pittsburgh, PA 15238
Visit our website at *www.rosedogbookstore.com*

ISBN: 979-8-89127-760-1
eISBN: 979-8-89127-258-3

The Accident

I was struck by a car in Denver, Colorado, and I was unconscious for five weeks, and when I regained consciousness, I had no memory of the accident or anything before the accident. My parents told me quite a bit about the accident, and in 1988 I obtained my medical records from both hospitals I was at. The copies of the medical record were discolored and difficult to read but I was able to read them using a magnifying glass and a dictionary. On the following page is a portion from the Children's Hospital medical record.

Due to the accident, I had a callus on my left side of my head, most of my right side of my body is partially paralyzed, and most of my left side of face is partially paralyzed including my left side of my tongue. I attended a handicapped school in Denver until my family moved back to Iowa. The school was named Boettcher School and located on 19th and Downing St. in Denver, Colorado, across the street from the Children's Hospital. There was an underground tunnel that connected Boettcher School with Children's Hospital, and during the school day students used the tunnel to go to therapy sessions at the hospital, myself included for three years.

According to the Boettcher School website the school opened in 1949 during the polio epidemic. In the winter of 1987–'88 I went back to visit the school and I was told by someone in the office that the school was closing at the end of the school year, and most of the students had already been transferred to regular public school. The only grade they had left at the school was kindergarten, but the kindergarten was also being closed at the end of the school year under the state policy of streamlining the students into regular public school. I recently looked up Boettcher

School on the internet and it stated that Boettcher School was demolished in February 1993.

Denver Children's Hospital
Medical Records

HISTORY: This 5-year-old white male was struck by an automobile on July 21, 1960. The patient was admitted to Denver General Hospital where a left depressed Parietal skull fracture was elevated by Dr. Thomas Craigmile. The brain was found to be edematous and contused but there were no epidural or subdural clots. There was a dural tear which was repaired by grafting. For several successive days while at Denver General this patient received I.V. Urea with apparently dramatic improvement and then was transferred here for convalescence.

PHYSICAL EXAMINATION: Revealed a well-developed, well-nourished, semi-comatose White male who gave no response to spoken voice. The left Parietal region showed a healing craniotomy scar. The skin was ecchymotic and edematous but the remainder of the bandage was not removed. The left eye was taped shut and the right eye was grade 1 in papilledema. The remainder of the physical exam was not essentially remarkable.

PROVISIONAL DIAGNOSES: Multiple skull fractures - Postdecompression. Cerebral edema.

LABATORY DATA: Hemoglobin was 11.1 grams, White blood count 12,600 with 72% granulocytes.

HOSPITAL COURSE: The patient was maintained for some time on tub feedings. He developed a Left corneal ulcer and was seen by Dr. Max Kaplan in consultation. The eye was treated with continuous dressings and Polyprion ointment with gradual healing of the ulcer. The patient's strength, especially in the right side where there had been a head-parses on admission, gradually improved and by the time of discharge he was able to speak a few single words. Several urinalyses remained clear. On one occasion a stool specimen was sent to the laboratory for possible parasitic infection but none was found. Following an 80-day hospital course the patient was discharged much improved.

FINAL DIAGNOSIS: Depressed Left parietal skull fracture. Cerebral contusion.

INSTITUTIONAL COMPLICATION: Corneal Ulcer.

CONDITION ON DISCHARGE: Improved.

My parents moved our family from Iowa to Denver, Colorado, in 1958 when I was three years old, and the house we moved to was the second house from the corner. My brother started kindergarten that autumn at the local Denver Public School. Sometime in 1959 or 60 I began to stutter, and my parents were told by the doctor that I would grow out of it. In the early part of 1960, my parents were considering moving the family back to Iowa but after the accident we stayed in Denver another nine years.

After I regained consciousness in the hospital, I had no memory of the accident or anything before the accident. I had a callus on the left side of my head; my right side of my body was partially paralyzed except for my right side of my mouth, right side of my tongue, my right nostril, my right eye and a small area around my right eye. My vision in my left eye was clouded, and most of the left side of my face is partially paralyzed including the left side of my tongue. The feeling on my left side of my face comes back on the lower part of my left side of my face.

After I regained consciousness, my parents began to talk to me about our house where we lived and about my brother and two sisters, hoping that I would regain my memory. They also told me that I was struck by a car. One day while my parents were visiting me, our next-door neighbors came to the hospital to see me, and at the time I still was not able to walk yet. As the neighbor's family waited in the hospital hallway, my parents were in my hospital room, putting me in the wheelchair and talking to me about the neighbors. They told me that they had a five-year-old son the same age as I was and that we were friends and ran around together, but when I came out of my room I did not recognize my neighbors.

In the next two hospital rooms there were two kids, and after breakfast I would be placed in a wheelchair, and I would go to the next two rooms and stay by the doorway and wake them up. This continued for a week or more until they were discharged. I do not know how that got started, but from my medical records, by the time I was discharged from the hospital I was able to speak a few single words, so I must have made a noise or pounded the doorframe to wake them up. As I remember they both hopped out of bed and were ready to go. Looking back, probably the hospital asked them to stay in bed until I woke them up, maybe the hospital thought a five-year-old patient needed some friends. One day the three of us were going to go to the hospital courtyard. As we were going down the hallway, a nurse stopped me and wanted to talk to me. I stopped to talk to the nurse while the other two kids went on without me.

About a week before I was discharged from the hospital, I was in therapy trying to walk, and my mom was there, and when I fell my mom told me that the hospital would not let me go home until I could walk. Since I had no memory of our home, the Children's Hospital was the only home I knew. When I was discharged from the hospital, I was able to walk but when I fell, I was not able to pick myself up, and I had to wear a helmet until the callus hardened enough to protect my head.

When I got home the first thing I wanted to do was walk around the backyard, and I fell three or four times outside, and someone had to come out each time to pick me up. When I walked around the inside of the house, when I got close to a piece of furniture, I would grab on to the furniture to steady myself. If you ever watch a baby learning how to walk the baby will do the same thing.

In the early 1960s the belief was that a person only uses 10 percent of their brain, and my parents were told that there was a possibility that another part of the brain would take control of my right side, but if my right side did not come back in three years it would take a long time, if ever, to come back. The Shriners organization paid for both my speech and physical therapy for three years, and the three years I had therapy I attended the Shriners Christmas party. When I was discharged from the hospital it was too late to start kindergarten, so I went to a sort of kindergarten that the Children's Hospital operated which lasted several months.

After I started walking halfway decent my parents forbade me to cross the street alone, which I obeyed for three years. But we had a slide in the backyard, and I was forbidden to climb the slide without someone going up with me. One day I decided to climb the slide by myself. I got all the way up to the top step of the slide. I stepped up on the slide with my left foot, raised my right leg, and my right foot hit the bottom of the slide. I made several attempts to raise my right leg, but each time my right foot hit the bottom of the slide. My next-door neighbors were watching me from their doorway and saw that I was having difficulty and called out that I should step up first with my right foot, and that is what I did. After I slid down the slide

I was proud of my accomplishment, and I ran into the house and told my mom what I did. I assumed that she would tell me that I could start climbing the slide by myself, but instead she wanted to see me do it again. I started up the slide again and she followed right behind me. Halfway up the slide I slipped but she was behind me, and she caught me, and that was the last time I tried climbing the slide for a while.

The following summer my parents moved the family to a house closer to the Children's Hospital and Boettcher School, and that autumn I started first grade at Boettcher School. The grades at Boettcher School went from kindergarten to twelfth grade, but it had less than two hundred students. Each year Mrs. Boettcher, the widow of the founder of the school, would give every student at the school five dollars and a box of chocolate candy the day before Christmas break for the first four or five years I was there. When the Shriners Circus was in Denver, each student was able to receive one free circus ticket.

Ever since I began walking halfway decent, I began pestering my parents, asking when I could start crossing the street alone. My parents finally told me, "As soon as the doctor says you no longer have to wear a helmet." My brother and later my sister had friends and classmates down the street or across the street and could cross the street anytime during the daylight hours, but I had to have someone go with me when I crossed the street. I did not know any of the kids in the neighborhood which were in my age group, and the students at Boettcher School came from all over Denver, so there were not any classmates within walking distance. I did not have any reason to cross the street, but it was just the idea that they could cross the street, and I could not.

When I was eight years old the doctor told me that I no longer had to wear the helmet, but even then my parents would not let me cross the street, but I started doing it anyway. I always told them after I returned where I went. There was a shopping center three blocks from our house and one of the stores was a drug store with a snack bar counter, and I would walk to the drug store and have a soda, then walk home. Eventually my parents accepted the fact that I was going to continue to cross the street. When I was about eight or nine years old I asked my mom, "If my callus is on my left side of my head, why is my right-side partially paralyzed?" She told me that the brain crisscrosses; the left side of the brain controls the right side of the body.

At Boettcher School there were cots on the second floor, and after lunch period the grade-school students would go to the second floor and have a rest period. There were two ways of going to the second floor, either by an elevator or a ramp. Most of the students used the ramp but I was required to use the elevator. After the doctor told me I did not need to wear the helmet I attempted to use the ramp, but the attendant that led the line of students up the ramp saw me in line and told me I needed to wear my helmet in order to use the ramp. I told her that the doctor said I no longer needed to wear my helmet, and she replied that I needed a note from my parents. As I got out of line and started walking towards the elevator the attendent began leading the line of students up the ramp, and I got in the back of the line and walked up the ramp.

When I reached the top of the ramp the attendant was standing near the top of the ramp watching everyone come up the ramp. When I passed her, she said nothing, and after that I continued using the ramp, and no one said anything to me. I can only assume someone in the office called my parents and got their permission for me to use the ramp.

When I was eight years old, I joined the local Cub Scout Pack, and after Cub Scouts I joined the Webelos, then the Boy Scouts. There are six merit badges in the Boy Scouts: Tenderfoot, Second Class, First Class, Star, Life, and Eagle, and when we moved back to Iowa in the summer of 1969 I had received my Star merit badge.

In the 1960s the Easter Seals organization operated a two-week summer camp in the mountains near Denver, Colorado, called Easter Seals Handicamp, which I attended for three summers in the mid-1960s. At the camp there was a swimming pool, arts and craft course, a nature course, horseback riding, fishing, and an archery and rifle range.

Eight years after the accident my dad began to talk to me about the accident, and from what he told me, on July 21,1960, he and I were about to cross the street near our house in Denver, Colorado. Dad saw the car coming and stopped and he thought I had stopped too, but I kept going, and by the time he saw me, I was halfway across the street. When he saw me in the middle of the street he yelled at me to run back, but I was struck before I could turn around. The accident bothered Dad all his life, and when he began talking to me about the accident, he told me that he always wondered if he had not yelled at me to run back maybe I would have made it across the street. As a Christian I believe that whatever happens, good or bad, happens by God's will. Even though I have had some mishaps I have always been able to survive, adapt, and move on.

The hood of the car came up to a peak in the center, and when the car struck me it knocked me off my feet, and the left side of my head hit the peak, and the peak acted like a knife. Then I was knocked thirty-five feet, hit the ground, and skidded another five feet, spun around several times, and began to shake violently for several moments, then became motionless.

When Dad ran over to where I landed, a piece of skull was missing, my left eye was open, and the area around my mouth was turning blue. Dad picked me up off the street and carried me to our neighbor's lawn, and a firefighter who lived across the street came over and began administering CPR until the ambulance arrived.

En route to the hospital I stopped breathing for nine minutes, and the hospital I was transported to had three neurosurgeons on call, but the hospital was only able to get a hold of the last neurosurgeon on their call list. When I arrived at the hospital I had a high fever, and I was packed in ice to lower my temperature to eighty-eight degrees; my medical records only state that I was placed in hypothermia. My dad told me that the hospital only had three cooling blankets and all three were in use. Several hours later I was stable enough to be taken into surgery. After I was taken out of surgery my parents asked the doctor if I had a fifty-fifty chance and the doctor told them my chances were one in a thousand. My parents also asked the doctor about putting a plate in my head to cover the area of skull that was missing, but the doctor at that time was concerned about a possible brain infection.

At the time of the accident the hospital I was at did not have an intensive care unit so my parents had to hire private nurses to watch me twenty-four hours a day. The way Dad described the nurses that my parents hired, they appeared to be off-duty nurses that worked at the hospital, so someone had to be at the hospital at the beginning of each shift to pay that nurse for that shift, or they would not start watching me. Several times when my parents came up to the hospital, they found me left alone and found the nurse in the cafeteria. I read up on the history of intensive care units on the internet, and according to the internet the concept of an intensive care unit in the United States began in 1950 during the Polio Epidemic; ten years later not all hospitals had one.

Three days after the accident my parents left the hospital for the night, and during the night my medical condition began to worsen, and eventually my medical condition worsened enough that the hospital called my parents and told them that they did not think I was going to make it. Dad told me that the hospital called them at four o'clock in the morning. By the time my parents and my aunt and uncle arrived at the hospital they had me stabilized, and six days later I was stable enough to be transferred to the Children's Hospital, and I was in the hospital a total of eighty days. My dad also told me that the doctor told him and Mom that due to the severity of the brain injury, they would not know how severe the brain damage was until I was in third grade. They were also told that Boettcher School was the second-best handicapped school in the nation. The best handicapped school in the nation was in Boston, Massachusetts. Dad told me that if Boettcher School had not been good enough that he and Mom would have been willing to send me to Boston. After I started first grade the doctor was amazed at how well I was doing in school. Dad also told me that due to the severity of my injury, my medical case was studied at UCLA Medical School in Southern California to study the methods that kept me alive.

In 1968 riots broke out in a number of cities, including Denver, and by the time our family moved to

Iowa in the summer of 1969, the grocery store and the drug store were the only two stores still open in the shopping center near our house. Our family moved to a farm near Mineola, Iowa, and in the autumn of 1969, I started ninth grade at Glenwood Junior High, in Glenwood, Iowa. At Glenwood Junior High I joined the FFA (Future Farmers of America), and for the next three summers I raised pumpkins.

My dad was an over-the-road truck driver and hauled produce for South Omaha Fruit Market in Omaha, Nebraska, and I sold all my pumpkins to the South Omaha Fruit Market. The year before I started raising pumpkins, there was an early frost in Colorado and it killed the pumpkin crops on the truck farms in Colorado, and pumpkin prices rose to eight cents a pound The first year I raised pumpkins the pumpkin prices had fallen to a penny and a half, and I had a half-acre of pumpkins that produced six thousand pounds of pumpkins. The second summer I had an acre of pumpkins, and the pumpkin prices jumped to two cents a pound, and the last summer I had an acre and a half, and the pumpkin prices that year were two and a half cents a pound.

I graduated from Glenwood High School in the spring of 1973, and that summer I worked at a temporary part-time job as a janitor at the Mills County Courthouse in Glenwood, Iowa, working twenty hours a week for ten weeks. After that job was over I found another job at the Glenwood State Hospital School in Glenwood, Iowa, taking care of residents on the ward. Since I only had the use of my left hand there were trivial things I was not able to do, like tie residents' shoes, so I would always have to have another co-worker tie the residents' shoes. When I found the job at the Glenwood State Hospital School, I was eighteen years old and had just recently entered the job market, and I had what I thought was a real concern that since I was disabled and had a slight stutter problem, which got worse in high-pressure situations, from a distance, someone might mistake me for a resident at the Glenwood State Hospital School.

After six months I found another job working for a company in Council Bluffs, Iowa, washing semi-trucks. During the four months I worked for the company there was a manager's meeting at the corporate head-quarters, and during the meeting they introduced a new policy. When our manager returned, he had an all-employee meeting to discuss the new policy. During the meeting he commented several times that after this meeting *one of you will quit*; I knew he was referring to me. The new policy was that it would only take fifteen to twenty minutes to wash a semi-truck, and it was taking me thirty to thirty-five minutes to wash a semi-truck. I continued to work there until I was laid off in July 1974.

I was out of work for three weeks until I found a job at the Nebraska Medical Center as a janitor. The three weeks I was unemployed I spent a lot of time at the Iowa Job Center in Council Bluffs, Iowa, and two days before I was hired at the Nebraska Medical Center I was at the Iowa Job Center looking into their computer for job openings and saw one that interested me. It was a clerical job, and it stated that *if hired, will be transferred to Washington, DC*. I was interested in traveling and seeing the rest of the country. I inquired about the job opening and was told the job was with the Federal Bureau of Investigation, and I made an appointment to be interviewed at the Omaha Field Office. Two days later I began working for the Nebraska Medical Center.

During the eight months from the time I sent in my application to the FBI and I was hired, the federal government had a hiring freeze. In the early spring of 1975, as I was waiting to clock in for work at the Nebraska Medical Center, my supervisor came up to me and told me that I was supposed to call the FBI office in Omaha. When I called the FBI office the person I talked to asked me if I was still interested in employment with the FBI. I told him yes, and he told me that they would send me a preemployment physical form my doctor would need to fill out, and an additional test I was required to take, which was an EEG (electroencephalogram). From what I read on the internet, an EEG measures electrical activity in the brain. That evening my supervisor came to the floor I was working on to see if everything was okay. I told her that I had applied for a job with the FBI before I started working there.

I started working for the FBI in Washington, DC, on April 22, 1975, and in November I was transferred to the Omaha Field Office. In the summer of 1979, I took a three-week vacation to the mountains, but before I left, my supervisor insisted that I put my license plate number into the computer, in the event my pick-up got pulled over for a traffic violation, and I was not in the pick-up. The field office would have a heads-up that something might have happened to me.

In February 1979 the Shah of Iran was overthrown, which caused the Iranian oil production to decrease, which caused a worldwide oil shortage. The governor of Colorado ran some tourist commercials on TV stating that potential tourists traveling through Colorado would be able to find gasoline. When I left on vacation I first went to Poncho Springs, Colorado, and took an overnight raft trip down the Arkansas River, then I went to the Grand Canyon in Arizona.

At the Grand Canyon my goal was to take a horse ride down the canyon. I did not have a reservation, but I assumed some tourists would be leery about traveling, due to the oil shortage, and cancel their reservations.

The morning after I had arrived, I checked the reservation desk to see if there were any cancelations and I was told that they could not allow anyone with a disability to take the horse ride down the canyon. That afternoon I took a free shuttle bus ride eight miles along the canyon, then I attempted to hike back to the hotel. I hiked about two or three miles then rested by a tree before continuing to hike a little further. As I was resting one of the free shuttle buses stopped and gave me a ride the rest of the way. After I left the Grand Canyon I drove to Las Vagas, Nevada, then up to Reno; then on the return home I stopped at the Salt Lake in Utah.

In January 1982 I had a CAT scan of my brain, and from what I saw it looked like if the brain was cut four ways. There would be the right-front, left-front, right-back, and the left-back, and it looked to me like the left-back of the brain was missing. That autumn I began taking some business courses at the local college. On February 3, 1983, I slipped on the ice at home and fractured my right hip while walking to my pick-up to go to a class at college, and the hip did not heal correctly. I received my associate degree in business mid-management in the spring of 1985, and in May 1987 I retired from the FBI on a disability due to the hip injury. Two years later I began working at a tourist resort in Wyoming, two miles from the east gate of Yellowstone National Park.

I started working at the resort in 1989, a year after the Yellowstone fires of 1988, and worked at the resort as a cashier at the gas station/grocery store during the summer tourist season for seven summers. It was interesting coming back each spring to see how the forest was recovering, and by the third or fourth year you could not tell there ever was a fire. In the autumn of 1993, after I left the resort for the season, I enrolled in college to receive my bachelor's degree in business, and in 1995 I graduated.

In January 1996 I began working at a truck stop in Council Bluffs, Iowa, as a cashier, and in the following year I took a vacation to Alaska in June 1997, and before I left, a co-worker at the truck stop asked me to send a picture postcard from Alaska to the truck stop. I drove to Bellingham, Washington, and placed my pick-up on a boat from Bellingham to Skagway, Alaska. At Skagway I drove north into part of Canada to connect to part of the Alaskan Highway in Canada known as the Alcan Highway. I took the Alcan Highway west into Alaska and eventually the Alaskan Highway split; the Alaskan Highway continued to Fairbanks and the other highway led to Anchorage. I took the other highway to Anchorage and turned off the highway to go to Valdez, and in Valdez I took a ten-hour glacier cruise.

After leaving Valdez I continued on to Anchorage then up to Fairbanks. After leaving Fairbanks I traveled north into the Arctic Circle and stayed at a resort called Coldfoot. At Coldfoot I bought a picture postcard and wrote a little note of where I was and addressed it to the truck stop. On the way to the post office to buy a stamp and mail the postcard, I accidentally dropped it between the cab and the box of my pick-up, and it did not fall to the ground so I bought another picture postcard wrote the same message, addressed it, and mailed it to the truck stop in Council Bluffs.

The following morning I left Coldfoot and traveled further north. I would have liked to have driven to the last resort, which was only ten miles from the Arctic Ocean, but I was running out of vacation time, so I traveled to the top of the timberline, then turned around and headed back to Fairbanks. The last resort was two hundred and fifty miles from Coldfoot, but the road I was on was called the Dalton Highway, but the Dalton Highway was just a gravel road. Sections of the Dalton Highway were built on the edge of the mountain, and there were no guardrails on those sections. As I was traveling I noticed a number of white crosses along the highway, and as I was nearing a section of the road near the edge of the mountain, I noticed a mud patch on the road. As I was going through the mud patch, my frontend of my pick-up began sliding to the edge of the mountain. I felt the frontend of the passenger side of my pick-up begin to tip down before the back tires grabbed some solid ground, and I was able to get back on the road.

Between Coldfoot and the end of the Dalton Highway there was only one gas station with a sign that read, "The next gas station 124 miles." I thought I had enough gas to make it, so I drove past the gas station. As I was nearing the end of the Dalton Highway, I ran out of gas a half mile from a gas station. I began walking to the gas station, carrying an empty gas can, but I only walked about fifty feet before someone stopped; they had some extra gas they gave me.

After I left Alaska, I drove into western Canada and spent two nights in Dawson City, Yukon. They were having their hundred-year anniversary of the Klondike Gold Rush. If I had more time I would've liked to of driven to Canada's Northwest Province, but I was running out of vacation time. After leaving Dawson City I traveled south to the Alcan Highway (Alaskan Highway in Canada) and took the Alcan Highway east, and it ended in Dawson Creek, British Columbia, and from there I took a highway southwest to Washington USA. About a month after I returned, I was working at the truck stop and I was told that the truck stop got an envelope from someone at the Air Force base near Fairbanks. Inside the envelope was my postcard that I accidentally dropped between the cab and the box of my pick-up; it fell to the ground on the Dalton Highway. The postcard also had a Post-It note on it stating where it was found.

In the following year I left the truck stop and returned to the resort in Wyoming, but due to road construction the tourist business was slow. Some travel agencies were recommending to their customers, who were planning to visit Yellowstone National Park, to go through the northeast gate, to avoid road construction. I left the resort after two months and began working at another truck stop in Council Bluffs, Iowa, as a cashier until I was hired at a casino in Council Bluffs as a cashier in November 1999.

In February 2002 I took another vacation to Alaska. I flew to Washington then took the Alaska State Ferry from Bellingham, Washington, to Ketchikan, Alaska, which was the first stop the ferry boat made. I stayed in Ketchikan for three days until the ferry boat returned, then I boarded the ferry boat to Juneau, Alaska. In Juneau, about an hour after I checked into a motel room, the desk clerk knocked on my door and told me that someone had called 911, and she thought it might have been me.

In Juneau I rented a car to drive around, and all the roads leading out of town eventually came to a dead end. Juneau is in the rainforest, and at that time of year Juneau was getting freezing rain every day for about ten to fifteen minutes, then shortly after it stopped raining, the ice would begin to melt off the streets. I stayed in Juneau four days, and during that time I drove around. One day I was driving on one of the roads that led out of town. I had a street map and I pulled off the road to check how far back the road went. The pullover area was a little lower than the road and ice covered. When I got through checking the map I put the car in gear, but the tires would only spin. I got out of my car to see which tire was spinning and noticed that the front tire on the driver's side had broken through the ice. I attempted to rock the car back and forth, but the car would not move. As I was trying to rock the car, two joggers came by and helped me get the car out. I worked at the casino in Council Bluffs for five years until I was laid off due to the installation of coinless slot machines, which reduced the number of money-handling people.

I was out of work for a year and a half until I found a job as a flagger at a construction company. During the year and a half I was out of work, I had my first book published, and I had a book interview write up from the local newspaper in Malvern, Iowa. The book was about the seventeen dominate countries in history that influenced the course of history, from Ancient Egypt to the United States. I worked for the construction company during the 2006 construction season, and the following summer I began working at a discount store in Shenandoah, Iowa, as a cart pusher.

When I first started I could only push in three or four carts at a time, but eventually I was able to push in thirteen or fourteen at a time, although company policy was that ten carts was the maximum you could push in at a time. Several times customers would come up to me while I was working and comment that "they should not make you have to push carts." I assume that management also was getting customer comments about having me push carts since management suggested several times to me that I should use the company computer to change my career preference to maintenance. I was a cart pusher for seven years, from 2007 to 2014, then I transferred to maintenance and worked in maintenance until my retirement in 2020. One of the duties assigned to maintenance was taking care of the redemption center cleaning and emptying the redemption machines. Since I have the use of only my left hand, when the redemption machine was full I had to ask another co-worker to tie up the bags.

In January 2009 I had a book interview at the local radio station in Shenandoah for my second book I had published. The book was about the history of the Middle East, from ancient times to the present. I had my third book published in 2019 and had another book interview at the local Shenandoah radio station. In the third book I merged some information from my first two books, plus new information. I had my fourth book published in 2022 and had a write-up in the local Glenwood, Iowa, newspaper. The book explores the rise and decline of the superpowers from Ancient Rome to the present. The United States became a superpower during World War II, as the United Kingdom began to decline.

References

Denver Children's Hospital
Medical record

Denver General Hospital
I was placed in hypothermia.

Boettcher School Website

My Parents, Mr. and Mrs. Carol and Mary Grudle